DULAC

Edited by David Larkin

Introduction by Brian Sanders

A Peacock Press/Bantam Book

Toronto * New York * London

An original Peacock Press/Bantam Book

DULAC

Copyright 1975 in all countries of the International Copyright Union
by Bantam Books, Inc.

All rights reserved.

PRINTING HISTORY:
Second Edition: December, 1975

This book may not be reproduced in whole or in part, by
mimeograph or by any other means, without permission in writing.
For information, address: Peacock Press, Bearsville, New York 12409, U.S.A.

Bantam Books are published by Bantam Books, Inc. Its trademark,
consisting of the words "Bantam Books" and the portrayal of a bantam,
is registered in the United States Patent Office and in other countries. Marca Registrada.
Bantam Books, Inc., 666 Fifth Avenue, New York, New York 10019, U.S.A.

Published simultaneously in the United States and Canada

PRINTED IN ITALY BY MONDADORI, VERONA

Edmund Dulac 1882-1953

Edmund Dulac was born in France, where, in his youth, he read law before turning to his true vocation by enrolling as a student at the art school of Toulouse. From there he went on to study further at the Académie Julienne in Paris. Between the years 1905 and 1918 he securely established himself as a very successful illustrator in both line and color work. During this period he had annual exhibitions in London which included his drawings for the ARABIAN NIGHTS. He settled permanently in London when he was thirty and became a naturalized British subject.

This book contains only a selection of his prolific output, but gives a clear picture of his genius, for it is my opinion, as an illustrator, that although he lived during an era when the profession abounded with talent, he was outstanding among his contemporaries who included such greats at Arthur Rackham, Howard Pyle and W. Heath Robinson. It is my pleasure now to note that Dulac's influence is again being shown in the work of several of the younger generation of today's illustrators and that this is contributing to the revival of the illustrated book.

My own acquaintance with Dulac's work stems from my childhood during World War II, when very few children's books were published in Britain, and consequently many of my generation read 'hand-ons' from the pre-war period. The glow that I received from his

illustrations to stories from Hans Andersen is one that I still remember today, when adult sophistication enables me to appreciate his drawings on another level. As a child, I saw only the picture that stimulated my imagination; today one is fully aware of the magnificent draftsmanship and elegance of composition that typify his work. The various influences in his drawings range from Mogul paintings through Japanese prints to the Pre-Raphaelites and his contemporary, the painter Gustav Klimt.

Dulac's images are set in a world of beauty. The content of his illustrations is never ugly, even his giants and monsters are decorated in a jewel-like manner. He avoids the trap of mawkishness, however,

usually with overtones of a marvelous humor. There is sensuality in many of his works and it is possible to think of publishing houses today that would balk at bare breasted females, complete with nipples, in children's fiction books. Present day Art Directors can learn from him that is is unnecessary to over-brief an artist. In many cases Dulac did not follow exactly the words of the passage illustrated, but instead distilled the sense of it to provide a better graphic embellishment to the page. For example, the text for the plate entitled 'He saw black eunuchs lying asleep,' from the ARABIAN NIGHTS, describes the eunuchs lying across the doorway with swords in their hands and the prince in the story has to step over them and pass through the silken hangings, before he learns what is beyond the doorway. Dulac has moved the eunuchs to the left side of the picture, a sword lies on the ground and the curtain has been opened to provide us with a glimpse of one of the maidens in the room, so giving a strong focal point to the drawing. The hero has been left out completely. Added are one pool, a fretted grille and superbly decorative textures to walls and floors. The result is a truly beautiful composition in which the artist's vision strengthens the written word. Dulac, I fear that were you alive today, the Art Editor would fail to see your point, revoke your artistic licence or at least endorse it with a number of alterations, none of which would improve your illustration.

The incident illustrated in a Dulac drawing is often made subservient to the background in order to enhance the image, with tiny people amid surroundings of succulent water-color washes. His use of water-color is the reason why a Dulac is so recognizable, although he is not afraid of breaking out from the constraints of the medium, as many of his originals are heavily worked with gouache body color. Students today wishing to be able to repeat his subtle textures will find it difficult owing to the lack of availability of the hand-made papers that he used. The subtlety of his originals was further improved in reproduction by the advent of the half-tone printing process. Many of his drawings were made to be reproduced from just three overlaid colors, red, yellow and blue. Where the artist in his

original used a black pen line, it could only be reproduced in printing by overlaying the full strength of all three colors. The result was a soft line which was never truly black. Dulac, of course, realized this limitation of the process and turned it to his advantage.

It is not only technique, however, that makes a Dulac. He can teach us much about pictorial construction, drawing and observation, for even in his stylizations these qualities come through. In his drawings, be the content flowers, objects, landscapes or people, the subject matter is always closely studied. Consider the mattresses in his illustration to the 'Princess and the Pea' and see what he has done with a variety of texture, color and line to make them real. The drapes

in the picture can almost be felt, the woodwork has grain, and the 'throw-away' of the candlestick partially cropped off in the foreground is as lovingly treated as the princess, whose figure takes up only a minute portion of the whole composition.

Even his caricatures and fantasies are rooted firmly in the real world from which he has gleaned his information. The Genie from the ARABIAN NIGHTS may be distorted, but his anatomy is very sound, as are the feathers and the structure of his wings. However, Dulac never allowed reality to overcome his sense of design. He never over-lit his subject matter, preferring to flatten out rather than dramatize the modeling with a strong light source. Horizons and foregrounds are brought onto the same plane by use of color, to produce a decorative and imaginative effect.

He reached his peak in the illustrations for SHAKESPEARE'S COMEDY OF THE TEMPEST, possibly because he was drawing for an adult readership, though he went on to work in nearly every area of the field of illustration, from making portraits and caricatures (some in the form of wax dolls) to designing sets and costumes for the theater, postage stamps, currency, medals, posters and playing cards. But it is in his book illustration, summarized here, that his true legacy to us lies.

BRIAN SANDERS

1) The Final Marriage Procession
Princess Badoura
A Tale from the Arabian Nights
HODDER & STOUGHTON

2) And there in its midst stood a mighty Genie
Arabian Nights
HODDER & STOUGHTON

3) Began to heap upon me terms of the most violent
and shameful abuse

Arabian Nights

HODDER & STOUGHTON

4) As he descended, the daylight in which hitherto he
had been travelling faded from view

Arabian Nights

HODDER & STOUGHTON

5) The Queen of the Ebony Isles
Arabian Nights
HODDER & STOUGHTON

6) He saw black eunuchs lying asleep
Arabian Nights
HODDER & STOUGHTON

7) The ship struck upon a rock
Arabian Nights
HODDER & STOUGHTON

8) After these, maidens on white horses, with heads unveiled, bearing in their hands baskets of precious stones

Arabian Nights

HODDER & STOUGHTON

9) On went the chariot, and King Pluto seemed greatly pleased to find himself once more in his own kingdom.

The Pomegranate Seeds
Tanglewood Tales

HODDER & STOUGHTON

10) Earth could not answer: nor the seas that mourn
In flowering Purple, of their Lord forlorn;
Nor heaven, with those eternal Signs reveal'd
And hidden by the sleeve of Night and Morn

Thirty-sixth Quatrain
The Rubáiyát of Omar Khayyam

HODDER & STOUGHTON

11) Oh Thou, who man of baser Earth didst make,
And ev'n with Paradise devise the snake:
For all the sin the Face of wretched man
Is blackwith—Man's Forgiveness give—and take!

Eighty-eighth Quatrain
The Rubáiyát of Omar Khayyam

HODDER & STOUGHTON

12) Act I Scene II
Miranda. O, the cry did knock
Against my very heart

Shakespeare's Comedy of the Tempest

HODDER & STOUGHTON

13) Act I Scene II
Prospero. A rotten carcass of a butt, not rigg'd.
Nor tackle, sail, nor mast...

Shakespeare's Comedy of the Tempest

HODDER & STOUGHTON

14) Act I Scene II
Prospero. Here in this island we arrived . . .

Shakespeare's Comedy of the Tempest

HODDER & STOUGHTON

15) Act I Scene II
Prospero. She did confine thee...
And in her most unmitigable rage,
Into a cloven pine

Shakespeare's Comedy of the Tempest

HODDER & STOUGHTON

16) Act I Scene II
Ariel. Full fathom five thy father lies;
Of his bones are coral made;
Those are pearls that were his eyes

Shakespeare's Comedy of the Tempest

HODDER & STOUGHTON

17) Act II Scene I
ARIEL

Shakespeare's Comedy of the Tempest

HODDER & STOUGHTON

18) Act II Scene II
Caliban. But
For every trifle are they set upon me

Shakespeare's Comedy of the Tempest

HODDER AND STOUGHTON

19) Act III Scene III
Ariel. You are three men of sin

Shakespeare's Comedy of the Tempest

HODDER & STOUGHTON

20) Act V Scene I
Prospero. Ye elves of hills, brooks
standing lakes and groves

Shakespeare's Comedy of the Tempest

HODDER & STOUGHTON

21) Act V Scene I
Prospero. And deeper than did ever plummet sound
I'll drown my book

Shakespeare's Comedy of the Tempest

HODDER & STOUGHTON

22) Act V Scene I
Ariel. Where the bee sucks, there suck I

Shakespeare's Comedy of the Tempest

HODDER & STOUGHTON

23) They grew until nothing but the tops of the
castle towers could be seen.

The Sleeping Beauty
**The Sleeping Beauty and Other Fairy Tales
from the Old French
Retold by Sir Arthur Quiller-Couch**

HODDER & STOUGHTON

24) The Good Merchant let drop the rose and
flung himself on his knees.

The Beauty and the Beast
Sleeping Beauty and Other Fairy Tales
from the Old French
Retold by Sir Arthur Quiller-Couch

HODDER & STOUGHTON

25) Soon they caught sight of the castle in the distance.

Beauty and the Beast
Sleeping Beauty and Other Fairy Tales
from the Old French
Retold by Sir Arthur Quiller-Couch

HODDER & STOUGHTON

26) She found herself face to face with a
stately and beautiful lady.

Beauty and the Beast

Sleeping Beauty and Other Fairy Tales
from the Old French
Retold by Sir Arthur Quiller-Couch

HODDER & STOUGHTON

27) These no sooner saw Beauty than they began
to scream and chatter.

Beauty and the Beast
Sleeping Beauty and Other Fairy Tales
from the Old French
Retold by Sir Arthur Quiller-Couch

HODDER & STOUGHTON

28) 'I have hardly closed my eyes the whole night! Heaven knows what was in the bed. I seemed to be lying upon some hard thing, and my whole body is black and blue this morning. It is terrible!'

Princess and the Pea

Stories from Hans Andersen

HODDER & STOUGHTON

29) One day he was in a high state of delight because he had invented a mirror with this peculiarity, that every good and pretty thing reflected in it shrank away almost to nothing.

The Snow Queen

Stories from Hans Andersen

HODDER & STOUGHTON

31) 'It is Gold, it is gold!' they cried.
The Snow Queen
Stories from Hans Andersen
HODDER & STOUGHTON

32) The Snow Queen sat in the very middle of it when she sat at home.

The Snow Queen

Stories from Hans Andersen

HODDER & STOUGHTON

33) Among these trees lived a nightingale, which sang so deliciously, that even the poor fisherman, who had plenty of other things to do, lay still to listen to it, when he was out at night drawing in his nets.

The Nightingale

Stories from Hans Andersen

HODDER & STOUGHTON

34) The Chamberlain goes in search of the Nightingale
The Nightingale
Stories from Hans Andersen
HODDER & STOUGHTON

35) Even Death himself listened to the song and said,
'Go on, little Nightingale, go on!'

The Nightingale

Stories from Hans Andersen

HODDER & STOUGHTON

36) The Merman King had been for many years a widower, but his old mother kept house for him; she was a clever woman, but so proud of her noble birth that she wore twelve oysters on her tail, while the other grandees were only allowed six.

The Little Mermaid

Stories from Hans Andersen

HODDER & STOUGHTON

37) But the Little Mermaid had no need to do this, for at the mere sight of the bright liquid, which sparkled in her hand like a shining star, they drew back in terror.

The Little Mermaid

Stories from Hans Andersen

HODDER & STOUGHTON

38) Then the Emperor walked along in the Procession under the gorgeous canopy, and everybody in the streets and at the windows exclaimed, 'How beautiful the Emperor's new clothes are!'

The Emperor's New Clothes

Stories from Hans Andersen

HODDER & STOUGHTON

39) I used to meet her in the garden, the ravine, and in the manor fields. She was always picking flowers and herbs, those she knew her father could use for healing drinks and potions.

The Wind's Tale

Stories from Hans Andersen

HODDER & STOUGHTON

40) He lifted it with a trembling hand and shouted with a trembling voice: 'Gold! gold!'

The Wind's Tale

Stories from Hans Andersen

HODDER & STOUGHTON